D1518998

The World of HORSES
CLYDESDALES

Lorijo Metz

PowerKiDS press

New York

To Melissa's dad, and Henry's coffee buddy, Larry Matson

Published in 2013 by The Rosen Publishing Group, Inc.
29 East 21st Street, New York, NY 10010

Editor: Amelie von Zumbusch
Book Design: Kate Laczynski

Photo Credits: Cover, p. 22 Peter Walton Photography/Photolibrary/Getty Images; p. 4 © iStockphoto.com/ Alan Crawford; pp. 5, 6, 16 iStockphoto/Thinkstock; pp. 6, 9 (bottom), 11 Joy Brown/Shutterstock.com; p. 7 Kenneth William Caleno/Shutterstock.com; p. 8 Jeff J. Mitchell/Getty Images News/Getty Images; p. 9 (top) Jason Edwards/National Geographic/Getty Images; p. 10 Kristofer Keane/Shutterstock.com; pp. 12–13 Paul McKinnon/Shutterstock.com; p. 14 © iStockphoto.com/Malcolm Fife; p. 15 Travel Ink/Gallo Images/Getty Images; p. 17 Bob Langrish/Dorling Kindersley/Getty Images; pp. 18–19 Margo Harrison/Shutterstock.com; p. 20 Cheryl Ann Quigley/Shutterstock.com; p. 21 Dirk Anschutz/Stone/Getty Images.

Library of Congress Cataloging-in-Publication Data

Metz, Lorijo.
Clydesdales / By Lorijo Metz. — 1st ed.
   p. cm. — (The world of horses)
ISBN 978-1-4488-7427-9 (library binding) — ISBN 978-1-4488-7500-9 (pbk.) —
ISBN 978-1-4488-7574-0 (6-pack)
1. Clydesdale horse—Juvenile literature. I. Title.
SF293.C65M48 2013
636.1′5—dc23

                          2011049579

Manufactured in China

CPSIA Compliance Information: Batch #WKTS12PK: For Further Information contact Rosen Publishing, New York, New York at 1-800-237-9932

Contents

Clydesdales

Have you ever seen a team of Clydesdales pull a wagon? Their huge hooves, covered in white, feathery hair, lift high off the ground with each step. Clydesdales are draft horses. Long before there were trucks, people used draft horses to pull heavy loads and plow fields.

Along with donkeys and zebras, all horses

The United States is home to the biggest number of Clydesdales. These horses are also common in Canada, Great Britain, New Zealand, and Australia.

Clydesdales are a breed, or kind, of horse. Some other well-known horse breeds are Arabian horses and Thoroughbreds.

belong to the horse family. One of the first animals in this family, which lived over a million years ago, was no larger than a fox. Today, a mighty Clydesdale may weigh as much as 2,000 pounds (907 kg). This is as much as some small cars weigh!

Most Clydesdales have white stripes down the center of their wide, flat faces.

Horses are measured in hands. One hand equals 4 inches (10 cm). Some Clydesdales stand 18 hands high from the ground up to their **withers**, or shoulders. This makes them taller than an average man.

Most Clydesdales are bay, or reddish brown with black manes and tails. Some are brown, black, and even chestnut. Chestnuts have reddish-brown coats, tails, and manes. All Clydesdales have long necks and large heads.

Clydesdales are probably best known for their feathers. These are the long hairs covering their huge hooves. Most Clydesdales have white feathers. However, Clydesdales with black legs sometimes have black feathers.

The white leg markings on this bay Clydesdale are known as socks. Many Clydesdale owners prize horses with white socks.

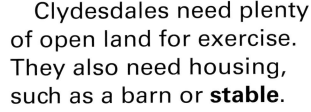

Clydesdales need plenty of open land for exercise. They also need housing, such as a barn or **stable**.

Daily **grooming** is important for Clydesdales. This includes brushing their coats, combing their manes and tails, and cleaning their hooves. Their feathers should be rinsed once a day and washed weekly.

An animal doctor, called a **veterinarian**, should visit a Clydesdale once a year.

There are special horse shampoos for cleaning a horse's coat, mane, and tail.

Clydesdales are known for their big feet. Their feet are about the size of a dinner plate!

Each Clydesdale should have its own space, called a stall, to sleep in. This stall should be filled with clean hay.

Veterinarians also look after a horse's teeth to prevent chewing problems.

Clydesdales wear shoes. Horseshoes are glued or nailed to the bottom of a horse's hooves. Since Clydesdales have big hooves, they need big horseshoes.

Gentle Giants

Draft horses eat almost twice as much food as smaller horses. A Clydesdale may eat up to 50 pounds (23 kg) of hay and 10 pounds (4.5 kg) of grains, mixed with molasses and **vitamins**, each day. They may also drink up to 30 gallons (114 l) of water each day!

Working with such large horses might be scary if they were not so gentle. People who work with Clydesdales often call them gentle giants.

Clydesdales eat several times throughout the day.

Clydesdales remain calm, even on busy streets full of people shouting and cars honking. Whether working with adults or children, they are always friendly and easy to handle.

Farmers often use troughs, such as the one these Clydesdales are drinking from, to provide water for their horses.

A mare is a female horse. A stallion is a male horse that can become a father. Mares carry their babies, or foals, for 11 months. Most Clydesdale foals weigh between 110 and 125 pounds (50–57 kg). Some weigh as much as 180 pounds (82 kg)! Male foals are called colts, while female foals are called fillies.

Clydesdale foals begin walking within a few hours. Soon they are drinking their mothers' milk. In the first few months, foals gain up to 4 pounds (2 kg) a day. By age three or four, they will have reached their full height. Clydesdales live about 20 years.

Clydesdale mares most often have one baby at a time.

13

The History of Clydesdales

Around 1720, a farmer from a part of Scotland called Lanarkshire **bred** a Flemish stallion with some of his draft horses. Flemish stallions were strong. They were also larger than draft horses. Knights often rode them into battle. The Flemish stallion and the draft horses had babies. These babies became the first Clydesdales.

The River Clyde flows through Lanarkshire, Scotland. In the past, Lanarkshire was known as Clydesdale. This is where the horses get their name.

This pair of Clydesdales is pulling a plow.

Scottish farmers began using Clydesdales to plow their fields. Later, coal miners used Clydesdales to pull wagons of heavy coal. In 1842, the first Clydesdales came to the United States. Many went to work on farms. Many also went to work in cities. Before cars, people often rode in **carriages** pulled by Clydesdales.

Carriage Training

Clydesdales that work together often wear matching tack.

Farmers now use machines, such as tractors, to do much of the work Clydesdales once did. While few Clydesdales plow fields today, many still pull carriages. Carriage training begins when a Clydesdale is about two years old.

To pull a carriage, a young Clydesdale must become comfortable wearing tack. Tack has several parts including a **harness** and a **bridle**. Harnesses connect, or hitch, the Clydesdale to the carriage. The bridle fits over the horse's head and connects to the **bit**. The bit is a metal piece that fits in the horse's mouth. Long straps called **reins** attach to the bit. The driver uses the reins to control the horse.

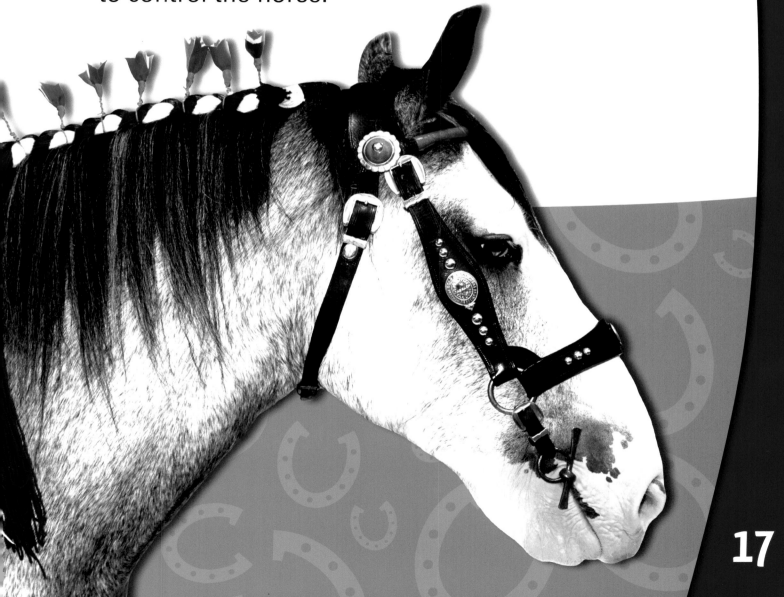

17

Today, Clydesdales pull carriages for show as well as work. In draft-horse shows, Clydesdales **compete**, or go up against other horses, in driving or hitch competitions. In hitch competitions, Clydesdales compete as teams pulling carriages. Judges rate them by how well they work together.

There are different classes, or types of competitions, for different-size hitch teams. A three-horse hitch team is called a unicorn. There are also four-horse, six-horse, and other sizes of hitch teams. In North America, one of the most famous draft-horse hitch competitions is the North American Six-Horse Hitch Classic Series.

Hitch teams are also known as hitches. It is important for the Clydesdales in a hitch to work well together.

19

While Clydesdales are best known for team competitions, they also compete in **breed** competitions, or horse shows. In the halter class, owners lead Clydesdales in front of judges. Much like a beauty contest, horses earn points for their looks. They also compete in riding, jumping, and dressage competitions. In dressage, Clydesdales complete a pattern of advanced moves.

These Clydesdales are owned by the Anheuser-Busch Companies. The horses are performing at Santa Anita Park, in Arcadia, California.

Clydesdales are also popular in parades, weddings, and at other special events. There is nothing like a team of Clydesdales, with manes and tails braided, pulling a fancy wagon in a parade. Clydesdales are known for pulling the Anheuser-Busch wagon. The Anheuser-Busch Companies own more than 200 Clydesdales.

By the 1930s, cars, trucks, and farm machines had begun replacing Clydesdales on farms and roads. Fewer people raised Clydesdales. Soon, these big horses were in danger of dying out.

Some people use Clydesdales instead of machines on small farms and for logging timber. This makes less pollution than using a machine.

Then, beginning in the 1960s, people began raising Clydesdales for horse shows and competitions. Today there are more than 5,000 Clydesdales in the United States, and their numbers are growing.

Glossary

bit (BIT) A metal part of a bridle that fits in the horse's mouth.

bred (BRED) To have brought a male and a female animal together so they will have babies.

breed (BREED) A group of animals that look alike and have the same relatives.

bridle (BRY-del) The part of a harness that fits over an animal's head.

carriages (KAR-ij-iz) Wheeled objects used to carry people or things.

compete (kum-PEET) To go against another in a game or contest.

grooming (GROOM-ing) Cleaning the body and making it appear neat.

harness (HAR-nes) The leather straps, bands, and other pieces used to hitch a horse or other animal to a wagon or plow.

reins (RAYNZ) Strips that attach to a bridle or bit and are used to direct an animal.

stable (STAY-bul) A building in which farm animals are kept and fed.

vitamins (VY-tuh-minz) Things that help the body fight illness and grow strong.

veterinarian (veh-tuh-ruh-NER-ee-un) A doctor who treats animals.

withers (WIH-therz) A place between the shoulders of a dog or horse.

Index

Websites

Due to the changing nature of Internet links, PowerKids Press has developed an online list of websites related to the subject of this book. This site is updated regularly. Please use this link to access the list: www.powerkidslinks.com/woh/clyde/